Dear Danny
Shari Rigby

Dear Danny

Shari Riggs

XULON PRESS

Xulon Press
2301 Lucien Way #415
Maitland, FL 32751
407.339.4217
www.xulonpress.com

© 2021 by Shari Riggs

All rights reserved solely by the author. The author guarantees all contents are original and do not infringe upon the legal rights of any other person or work. No part of this book may be reproduced in any form without the permission of the author.

Due to the changing nature of the Internet, if there are any web addresses, links, or URLs included in this manuscript, these may have been altered and may no longer be accessible. The views and opinions shared in this book belong solely to the author and do not necessarily reflect those of the publisher. The publisher therefore disclaims responsibility for the views or opinions expressed within the work.

Printed in the United States of America

Paperback ISBN-13: 978-1-66282-196-7
Ebook ISBN-13: 978-1-66282-199-8

Dedicated to my friend
Sue,
Who loved as best she could

Preface

Dear Danny,

Though we have never met, your mom and I were good friends many years ago. Our friendship began in 1973 when Sue and I worked together. At the time, she had a four-year-old son, Jeff, and since I didn't have children of my own yet, being around a young child was a new experience for me. being with the two of them proved to be delightful.

By the time you were born in 1998, your mother had changed emotionally and mentally from the person I once knew. Sue had you late in life, and even as excited as she was about being a mom again, it wasn't easy for her. She'd encountered many struggles and endured much heartache over the years that took a significant toll on her. My heart goes out to you because, through no fault of your own, it seems you got the short end of the stick, proving that life can be unfair.

I wish you could have known your mom when she was younger - before being dealt such a difficult hand. Joy filled her, and she was never without a smile on her face.

Until Jeff died.

The shock of losing him was overwhelming, and it took years for her grief to subside. Through the next two decades, she struggled through two divorces, adding to her pain.

The final blow fell when your dad died of a massive heart attack at the age of forty. It was simply too much for your mother to bear, and she took a downward spiral, making your life miserable.

Thank God for your Aunt Misty and her family. She and your uncle and their daughters have been there for you, loving you unconditionally as you've grown into a man.

I recently stumbled over a memoir Sue and I worked on years ago but never finished. Misty and I have kept in touch, so I contacted her to find out what she thought about my completing it. She was all for the idea - mainly because she hoped it would be a way for you to know your mom as she once had been. I couldn't agree more.

Here's her story.

Shari

PART I
A Mother's Story

Chapter 1

I looked at the clock again, probably for the fourth time in ten minutes. Only 4:50.

Why is time dragging? I still have forty minutes before I can leave work.

Betty walked up. "The day's almost over, Sue." Glancing at me, she asked, "Hey, you usually have a smile on your face about this time of day. Is something wrong?"

"Oh, I feel kind of uneasy for some reason. I can't put my finger on it, but this sense of urgency to go home won't leave me."

"Why don't you go? It's only a few minutes."

"You know what? I'm going to. I can't get any work done feeling like this," I said while putting on my sweater. It was a cold, cloudy day in late November. "I know I'm just being silly. I'll see you tomorrow, Betty."

I started speeding as soon as I got on the freeway. *This is ridiculous. Why does it seem so important for me to be home? Calm down. It's probably nothing. Don't drive so fast; you'll get home a lot sooner if you're not in an accident.*

I drove by the house and noticed that my husband, Steve, wasn't home yet, which meant it was up to me to pick up Jeff from the babysitter.

Well, Jeffy, once we get home, we can start making dinner and have it all ready for your dad. I was trying to calm myself by planning a pleasant evening with my family. *Even if your dad has to work late, we can still make that pizza we planned on and have a great time, just the two of us.*

Thinking back to early that morning, I could picture Jeff stumbling out of bed, rubbing his eyes. As was our habit since I'd gone back to work, my son would sit on my lap to wake up. I'd kiss and hug him for as long as he'd let me, and then we'd get ready for the day. I'd usually ask him a few questions, which he thought were silly most of the time. Today, I'd asked him what the date was.

"It's Wednesday," he said, giggling.

"Right, Smarty Pants, you know what day of the week it is. What's the actual date?"

Dear Danny

"November 30, 1977. Geez, Mom. I'm not a baby, I'm eight-years-old. I can even tell you my address and phone number if you want!" He had a smirk on his face, letting me know he was teasing.

"You're *my* baby, and you always will be." I tousled his hair, which I loved to do. It was thick and blond and usually a mess. And those eyes - deep blue and full of mischief. Being outside playing was his favorite thing to do. My son was all-boy. I wondered how much longer we'd have these special moments together. "Okay, Kiddo. Time to get going."

He raced to the car, always in a hurry. On the other hand, I wasn't in that much of a rush. I hate saying good-bye to my little guy, even if it was only for a day. I wished I could be a stay-at-home mom, but it simply wasn't in the cards for Steve and me. Neither of us had gone to college, and while we both had pretty good jobs, we lived paycheck-to-paycheck.

We'd recently gotten married after living together for a few years. Jeff had started asking why our last names were different, so we agreed it was probably time to tie the knot. Jeff looked just like Steve, even though he wasn't my boy's birth father.

It was kind of funny. Even though not blood-related, they shared the same gorgeous blond hair and build. They looked so much alike that no one ever questioned their relationship. That, coupled with the tender love they shared, sealed the deal in my eyes. Nope - there was no question. Steve was Jeff's dad.

Jeff waited for me before getting into the car, knowing the drill. Hugs and kisses before saying goodbye. We still had to drive to the babysitter's, but Jeff was in too much of a hurry to give me the time of day once we arrived there. His friends would be waiting for him, and before long, they'd all get on the school bus together. I'd go on to work, about a half-hour away.

Chapter 2

By now, I'd arrived at the babysitter's house. She and I had been friends for a long time. As I pulled into the driveway, her husband came out and met me. I looked around but noticed there were no kids playing outside. Odd. Before I had a chance to say anything, he told me that Jeff had fallen off his bike a few minutes earlier, and that Samaria had taken him to the emergency room at a nearby hospital.

"Why didn't you call me?"

"There was no time. Now, don't worry, Sue, he's fine. It's just a little bump on the head. We wanted to take every precaution, so my wife took him to the E.R. She'll be waiting for you there."

Pulling out of the driveway, I started shaking. "Okay, Sue, stop it!" Now I was yelling at myself. *It's probably just a cut or bruise. Maybe he'll need a couple of stitches. But you've got to calm down. It's nothing serious. Kids fall off bikes every day.* The hospital wasn't far away, and I knew where to go once I arrived, having visited the E.R. when we thought Jeff had broken his arm. I ran into one of the medical staff in the lobby. "I'm looking for my son. Can you tell me where he is?"

"Certainly, ma'am." She led me to the receptionist who, after checking her list, pointed out a little room where my sweet boy lay all alone on a gurney. He turned his head, recognizing me. He looked terrified.

With a small pained voice, Jeff started crying. "Mom. Mom." He looked up at me wide-eyed with fear and needed me to comfort him. Horrified, I realized I should have been here with him instead of at work.

A nurse entering the room explained Jeff had fallen and hit his head. "He's feeling nauseous and sleepy, so we're keeping a close eye on him."

Then I noticed Samaria was there. "Sue, I'm so sorry. They were just playing outside."

She looked frazzled and close to tears. I tried to encourage her, insisting she had done the right thing by bringing him here. The details of what had happened seemed unimportant at that moment. I turned my attention back to Jeff when a doctor came in. He introduced himself as Dr. Haravey and then began gently examining my little boy's trembling body.

It bothered me that Jeff seemed so dazed and incoherent. "How serious is it, doctor?"

"Well, there's no reason for us to be alarmed. Your son probably has a concussion, but we're not going to know anything until we take some X-rays. You'll have to wake him up every fifteen minutes until we can take him down the hall."

"Oh, no! I don't have a watch. I won't know when it's time."

With a slight smile, he said, "Don't worry, I'll help you. I'll let you know when enough time has passed. I've got some other patients to tend to, but will check in with you every few minutes."

The door closed behind him, and I noticed Samaria had left. Now it was just the two of us surrounded by hospital equipment. Everything felt so surreal, and I prayed I'd wake up from this nightmare soon.

I bent over close to his face. "What happened, honey? What were you doing?" He looked small and helpless as I brushed his hair back.

"Mom. Mom, it hurts. My head hurts."

His eyes appeared glazed over, kind of foggy. "Jeff, can you see me?"

"Yes. Mom --"

He dropped off to sleep before he could finish his thought, so I shook him gently. He had to stay awake longer than that.

"I'm here, Jeff. Try not to be scared. I'm right next to you. You need to stay awake. I know you're sleepy, but you have to try."

"I'm tired - I can't --"

"Jeffy. Wake up, Jeff!" I yelled at him. "Tell me what happened."

"I fell - crashed."

He nodded off again.

The doctor tapped on the door and stuck his head in. "Sue, it's been fifteen minutes."

"He woke up - barely. He told me his head hurt. It's so hard for him to stay awake. His eyes are glazed, and I'm not sure how well he can see me."

The doctor couldn't help but notice how frightened I was. "I know it's difficult not to worry, but you have to do your best."

"Do you have any idea what happened? I was at work, and he was with the babysitter. I saw her for a brief moment, but not long enough to find out anything."

"We haven't gotten a complete picture yet as to exactly what occurred. We've heard that Jeff was riding his bike or skateboard, and for some reason, fell. I'm sure the babysitter knows more by now."

"I'll have to call her later."

"Keep talking to him. I'll be back," he said, leaving the room.

I searched Jeff's little body while he slept. I knew every inch of him and how he should be. *What is this bump? His whole forehead is protruding. Why didn't I notice that before?* My heart started beating wildly.

He began thrashing around.

"Oh, Jeffy," I moaned, attempting to hold him down while hugging him. Maybe I could take some of his pain away. *He's getting less and less coherent when he wakes up.* My pulse continued to race. Even though the doctor had just left, I kept looking for someone to come in.

Where is everyone? Somebody needed to be in this room, helping my boy. I looked around at the pale green walls and squeezed my eyes shut. *Don't cry, Sue. If you do, you'll lose all control. Keep talking to him. Remember, you've got to keep talking.*

"Christmas is coming soon. What do you want this year? We'll have to start making a list and also figure out what we want to get Dad. Do you know what he wants? I love you, Jeff." *Please be all right! You have to be okay.*

"Mom --" His voice, so small, carried such pain.

"I'm here, honey, right next to you. I'm not leaving." *I'll never leave you.*

"Mom, where am I?"

His words were beginning to slur, making it difficult to understand him, but at least he was trying.

"There's been an accident. You're in the hospital, and the doctors are going to help you."

"I'm scared," he whimpered.

"I know, honey. I know. But everything's going to be alright." I spoke soothingly. It took a conscious effort to keep my voice from faltering.

I began humming one of our favorite songs while massaging his hands and arms over and over, back and forth. Watching him lying there was difficult. I wanted him to talk to me. But awake, the pain consumed him, so I decided to try and let him sleep. I kept humming and talking and got some groggy responses, but only for a few seconds at a time.

After what seemed to be an interminable amount of time, the doctor and a couple of the nurses showed up.

"We're going to take Jeff to X-ray. We shouldn't be too long. Perhaps now would be a good time to fill out the necessary insurance papers. Get a cup of coffee or something. You need to unwind a bit." The doctor placed his hand on my shoulder. It felt good having someone tell me what to do. It was as if he removed some of the heavy burdens by merely touching me. But most importantly, something was finally being done for my son.

"All right. But I want to know when he's finished. Maybe I'll just bring a cup of coffee back here to the room."

"That's not necessary. We have an intercom system here. If we don't see you right away, we can page you. Go and get some fresh air."

I turned back to Jeff. "You're going to go with the doctor and nurses for a little while. But don't worry. I'll be waiting for you. You're going to be just fine." I had to say those words over and over. "You're going to be fine. Everything will be alright." I needed to convince myself even more than Jeff.

Chapter 3

Since I didn't know where to go to fill out the appropriate papers, I headed to the main desk.

"My son is in the emergency room having X-rays taken. I'm sure there are forms to complete, so I might as well get it done now. Can you tell me where I need to go?"

"Yes, ma'am," she said, pointing. "Straight across, through that doorway."

I did my best to fill out the papers and then looked up at the attendant sitting there. "I'm sorry. My husband isn't here yet, and I don't know his social security or insurance policy numbers. Can I take these with me?"

"Just fill out what you can, and we'll get the rest of the information later. No need to worry."

No need to worry. This woman had no idea what she was saying to me. I had every reason to worry. My son - my life - was in the hospital in severe pain after falling on his head. I wanted to scream at her, "How dare you say those words to me?"

Instead, I finished the paperwork to the best of my ability and then left for the cafeteria. It soon became apparent it was quite a distance away, so I changed my mind, heading to the emergency waiting room. Chairs were lined along the walls. I sat alone staring mindlessly at the television while my thoughts raced.

Jeff's eighth birthday was just a month ago. We threw a big party - his first - and when he got up that morning, he bounced up and down.

"Happy birthday, Buddy!" Steve had thrown Jeff's bedroom door open, and we stood there watching him, laughing.

"I'm eight, I'm eight-years-old now, and I get to have a party today!" His joy knew no bounds.

"That's right," I said. "But we have to get moving if we want to get to grandma and grandpa's house to help decorate and be there when everyone arrives." The celebration was going to take place in my parents' backyard.

Dear Danny

We'd never seen him so happy. Watching him play with all his friends - and there were so many - was a delight. I'm not sure who was smiling more, Jeff or me. We'd bought him a birthday cake - again, his first, since I'd always made them at home. There were balloons all over the yard and lots of games to play, and when it was time for him to open his presents, I laughed out loud. He was giddy with excitement. Steve looked at me and said, "Wow - I don't think we'll ever get this kid to go to sleep tonight." I had to agree, but it would be such a small price to pay.

Someone walked into the room, and I was back in the present. *I've got to reach Steve. He won't know where we are.*

I found a payphone and tried calling him, but he didn't answer. Then I remembered he'd mentioned earlier that he'd be late getting home because of a mandatory meeting after work. *I know. I'll call his parents. They live close to us. Maybe they'll watch for him.*

Steve's dad, Roger, answered the phone, and I told him where Jeff and I were. Not wanting to worry him, I held in the tears that I knew he'd be able to detect in my voice. As light and breezy as I could, I went on to explain that X-rays were being taken and there was no reason for him or my mother-in-law to come to the hospital.

"I'm sure it's just a concussion, so please don't worry. I can't reach Steve because he's not home yet. Will you look out for him?"

"Sure, Sweetheart. But are you positive you don't want one of us to come there? It would only take five minutes."

"No, I don't want to bother you. I'm sure it's nothing serious. If you can let Steve know, though, I'd appreciate it. Talk to you soon." Returning to the waiting room, I sat down.

Oh, I really should get a hold of my mom. She's gonna freak out when she hears Jeff and I are at the hospital.

Thank goodness, Dad answered.

"Hi, Dad. I'm at the hospital with Jeff because he fell off his bike. Right now, they're taking X-rays of his head." My voice started shaking. "I'm not sure why I called you guys. I guess I don't want to admit it, but I'm scared."

"What offramp do we take? We'll be there right away. Just sit down and try not to worry."

"But, Dad, I don't think it's necessary."

"Where's Steve?"

"I'm not sure, but I think he had a meeting after work."

"Okay. Hang in there. We'll only be a few minutes."

Relief flooded me. Before too long, my parents would be here, and I wouldn't have to do this alone any longer.

My thoughts drifted back to 1969.

Chapter 4

Sixteen years old and pregnant, and still two more years of high school ahead of me. What was I going to do? Had I ruined my life? Mom sure thought so; in fact, she told me I should get rid of the baby. There are no words to express the anger and fear I felt. Not just because of being pregnant, but how could Mom - my sweet, loving mother - ever suggest such a thing as abortion? I had friends who'd done it. But it was illegal, not to mention immoral. No, I couldn't do that, no matter what my mother said.

I guess I couldn't blame her. My gosh, I hadn't even gotten my driver's license yet. What made me think it would be possible to take care of a baby? A whole other person, for heaven's sake. That's more responsibility for me than my new puppy - which I ignored.

Well, I won that argument. I refused to go to the abortion clinic. But Mom then insisted that my boyfriend James and I get married. What a joke that turned out to be. We had a ceremony and moved in with his folks. I don't think it took even six weeks before I was back home. I hated living with him.

Those next few months flew by. Going to school and preparing my life for a new baby kept me busy, and before I knew it, he was born.

Any pain I experienced while giving birth was forgotten as soon as I laid eyes on my son. Jeffrey. He was beautiful, and Mom fell in love with him instantly too. Yep, that's how things started, and surprisingly, I adored being a mommy, even from the get-go.

Chapter 5

I came out of my reverie when someone walked up to me. "Roger! What are you doing here?"

"I just had to come, Honey," he said. "I'll wait with you."

I stood and gave my father-in-law a long hug. How nice to no longer be alone.

"So, what's going on?"

"He's in X-ray now, so I'm just waiting." Tears came to my eyes as I explained what we thought had happened. "I guess he was riding his bike or skateboard with some of his friends at the babysitter's and fell. We still don't know the facts. I think once things settle down here, I'll ask to talk to one of the kids who were there. Either that or have Samaria find out for me."

We sat together quietly.

"Everything's going to be fine, you know?" Roger finally said. I nodded my head, wanting to believe him. "Oh, there's my mom and dad!" Seeing Mom, I broke down crying, and she took me in her arms. "Oh, honey, I'm so sorry. Do you know anything yet?"

Roger reached his hand out to my parents, "Audrey, Frank, good to see you."

We all sat down, and I repeated what I'd just told Steve's dad. "It sure seems like it's taking a long time to finish with the X-rays," I muttered. Mom drew me closer to her. "It probably feels like everything's in slow motion, doesn't it?"

I nodded.

"It shouldn't be much longer," Mom said reassuringly.

Taking a deep breath, I was just about to say something when the doctor showed up.

He explained that Jeff did have a concussion and would be admitted to the hospital for close observation. I shuddered, and the doctor noticed.

"It's going to be a long night, but we'll get through it, and hopefully, he'll be more cognizant tomorrow morning. Right now, you need to go to the admissions office and get that taken care of," said Dr. Haravey.

I looked at my mom, and both of us took a deep breath. "I'll go with you," she said.

Entering the office, we couldn't help noticing that the clerk was busy. Ultimately turning around, she took some information from me and then asked, "Do you know where the intensive care unit is?"

"What? What are you talking about? Nobody said anything to me about intensive care!"

"They didn't tell you?"

"Tell me what?"

Mom stepped in. "Now, wait a minute. You'd better get your stuff together and call a doctor down here to explain what's going on. Her son is hurt, and nobody said anything about ICU."

"Certainly." The clerk picked up the phone and told someone to send Dr. Haravey to the admitting office right away. "He'll be here momentarily," she said softly, motioning for us to have a seat.

The doctor was apologetic. "Sue, I'm sorry. I should have told you that anyone with a head injury is automatically sent to intensive care, especially if they're sleepy. It's perfectly normal." His tone helped reassure me. "Thank you, Dr. Haravey. It helps to know that."

"Well, again, I'm sorry not to have explained it earlier," he said, turning to leave.

After we found out how to get to the ICU, Mom hugged me and said that she, Dad, and Roger were going home but would be back first thing in the morning. "Since it's so late and nothing much should be happening over the next few hours, we'll be able to get some sleep. I know you'll be here all night, but try to get some shut-eye yourself. Be sure and give us a call if you need to before morning, okay?" I gave her a lingering hug, trying to get all the strength I could from her.

I looked around the area, assessing it. The fact that each patient had their own room comforted me. At least he had privacy. The walls were a soft yellow, which I assume was an attempt to be calming. But the medical staff rushing here and there to care for their patients - all in serious condition - quickly reminded me where I was.

Jeff's appearance drew my attention before I could greet the nurse. It was apparent his pain had become more intense than when I'd last seen him in the emergency room. Now he was flailing around. I stood there, stunned. The nurse turned to me and explained Jeff would have to be restrained to the bed to keep him from hurting himself. My heart broke. Seeing my baby like this was unbearable.

"Why can't he be given pain medication or something?" I asked the nurse.

"We can't give him anything yet. Doctor's orders. Head injuries are tricky, and we have to be very careful." Every inch of my body screamed from pain, but still, I wished I could trade places with him.

Before completely restraining him, he sat straight up. "Please, Mom! Please help me," he cried.

"Jeffy, you've got to lay still. They're trying to make it better, but they can't when you're moving around so much." My voice choked.

"Keep talking to him, Sue," the nurse said. "He needs to hear your voice."

"I love you, Jeff. Everything's going to be okay. I'm here." I repeated this time and again. He would lay still for a few seconds, then open his eyes and fretfully look around. Just as quickly, he'd fall asleep again. Those moments of semi-consciousness were occurring quite often now. Dr. Haravey came in more frequently to note Jeff's actions and reactions.

His attempts at trying to rouse Jeff were proving fruitless.

I must have beome hysterical because the next thing I heard was the doctor yelling, "Susan. Susan. He can't hear you. Stop it!" Looking around at the nurses, he nodded to one of them, and she gently led me away from Jeff and into the ICU waiting room.

Chapter 6

I'd been dozing for about an hour when Steve made it to the hospital and found me. The only thing he was aware of at that moment had come from a note left on our front door by his dad, telling him Jeff and I were at the hospital.

Right away he started throwing questions at me. "What happened? Why didn't you call me? How long have you been here?"

Still groggy, I told my husband that I'd called him several times, but he hadn't answered. I explained we were here because Jeff had an accident at the babysitter's, and he was being observed in intensive care because he'd suffered a head injury.

"How is he? Can we go see him?" Steve pulled at me frantically. He was frightened and didn't know what to think. It reminded me of the look on Jeff's face when I first arrived at the hospital. Leading Steve to the ICU, he broke away from me and barged through the doors. I knew the rule in this unit was to call from the wall phone first to be let in, but he didn't give me a chance. I hadn't been able to forewarn my husband of what to expect before he got to Jeff. The sight of his son restrained to a bed thrashing around was too much for him to take in, and I saw tears streaming down his cheeks.

Dr. Haravey stood next to Jeff's bed and started explaining his condition to Steve. His soothing demeanor helped calm my husband's anxiety, which, in turn, helped me.

"He needs to know you're here, Steve. Can you think of some things you could talk about that the two of you enjoy doing together?"

I reminded Steve of their love of all things football. The two of them had something going where he had taught Jeff how to bet on the game by watching the odds in the newspaper. They'd started betting on which team they each thought would win. The loser of the bet had to clean up after our Irish Setter's messes in the backyard. Jeff was surprisingly holding his own and often won.

Watching his dad pick up dog poop after losing, tickled our son to no end.

"Maybe that could jostle something deep inside him. Try it, Steve," I said.

My husband looked around, not completely understanding the purpose, but he wanted to help in any way he could. "Hey, Jeff. Remember the last Raiders game we watched? You sure beat the heck out of me. I can still hear you laughing at your old man."

No sign from our little boy that anything registered with him.

"Can you tell me the name of the Dallas Cowboys' quarterback? What about Oakland?"

Jeff's eyes opened for a moment, and he answered Steve's questions. Maybe the fact that his dad's voice was more authoritative than mine helped. I couldn't help crying seeing Jeff's response. Then, just as quickly, he slipped back into sleep. Steve and I spent the rest of the night taking turns talking to him hourly. We were exhausted by the time the sun came up.

Chapter 7

Our parents showed up early that morning, much earlier than I expected. One of them must have called the hospital at some point and found out Jeff's condition was worsening because I'd not phoned anyone.

"Oh, Mom. I can't stand this. What are we going to do?"

"I know. I can't imagine how excruciating it is for you to be going through this and seeing Jeff in such a state. Do you think it might help if we grandparents went in and saw him?"

"They just took him to X-ray or somewhere to have scans taken, so we're waiting on that."

Dad asked if Steve and I had notified work yet. I honestly hadn't thought about it, but he was right. Calling the office, I spoke with my friend Annie, telling her not to worry. "Concussions happen all the time to active little kids, but hopefully, we'll know more soon."

We all sat waiting in the lobby. I'd lost any sense of time, so I'm not sure how long we'd been there when Dr. Haravey had us paged. We were to meet him in the hall near the X-ray department. Our parents squeezed our hands and we made our way to the doctor.

He matter-of-factly explained the severity of Jeff's injuries. He had a fractured skull, and a large blood clot that had developed. Both of us were dumbstruck. I couldn't utter a word.

Steve finally asked, "What do you think we should do?"

Dr. Haravey minced no words. "There's no question this is an emergency. We have to remove the pressure caused by the blood clot immediately. That's the cause of Jeff's pain."

"Do what you have to do," my husband choked out. "Our son's life is in your hands."

I couldn't grasp the intensity of the situation. *Why can't they just give my boy some medicine and make it better?* Steve put his arm around my shoulders and we returned to the waiting room to give our parents the news.

All of their faces turned white when Steve told them what the doctor had said. "The surgery is supposed to take at least four or five hours." His hands shook, and it became apparent he needed to sit down.

My mom was the first to be able to put words together. She looked at us and said, "Now would be the best time for you guys to go home, shower, and put on some comfortable clothes. We're all going to be here for a while."

Her words were more of an instruction that we should follow rather than a suggestion. Since neither of us could make a decision, we nodded to each other and stood up to leave.

"Are you guys okay to drive?" my father-in-law called after us.

As soon as he heard his dad's voice, Steve seemed to let go of his anxiety and answered, "Yeah. We'll be fine." He took hold of my hand as we left the hospital.

Chapter 8

The two of us said nothing on the drive home. Once there, we went straight to our bedroom and sat down on the bed together. Steve reached out for me, and we fell into each other's arms, crying and hugging while holding onto each other for dear life. We shared something unspeakable, and no words were necessary.

Steve got up to take a shower, and I followed close behind. We stood underneath the running water together, not wanting to be apart for even a minute. Afterward, we threw on our clothes and made our way back to the hospital.

My mom and dad looked up. "Oh, good, you're back," she said. "Those clothes look much more comfortable than what you still had on from work."

"Have you heard anything yet?"

Mom answered me, "No, but it's only been a couple of hours. Have you two eaten anything?"

I shook my head. "I'm not hungry and not sure I could keep anything down if I did eat."

Steve's dad jumped in. "Well, you need something in your stomachs. We'll run to the cafeteria and see what we can find."

Though not comprehending what he said, I nodded my head. "So, I guess we just sit here," I said to no one in particular.

We waited. And waited. And waited, eventually hearing that Jeff was in recovery and everything had gone as well as possible. But before anyone could take a breath, we caught a glimpse of doctors and nurses running down the hallway, pushing Jeff's gurney towards intensive care. It was so quick, my dad questioned whether or not it was his grandson.

All on our feet now, I quietly murmured, "It was Jeff. Did anyone else see the bandages around his head?" Before anybody could answer me, Dr. Haravey appeared.

"During surgery, Jeff fell into a coma. It sometimes happens with severe trauma to the brain. That, coupled with the anesthesia, it hasn't been possible for us to wake him up. Before you go in and see him, you need to know he's on a respirator to help him breathe." The doctor's demeanor was sullen.

"Are you saying he's on life-support?" Mom asked.

Dr. Haravey nodded. "It'll be a few minutes before you can see him, and then my nurse will come get you."

Horrified, none of us moved until my mom grabbed me and held on tight.

"What's he talking about? I'm not sure I even know what a coma is," I sobbed.

"Yes, you do, Sue," said Steve. "He's in a deep sleep and can't wake up."

"For how long? It can't be for long, can it?" My mind refused to understand what I was hearing. "Oh, my God! Some people are in comas for years, aren't they?"

No one said anything else as we all hugged each other and cried.

Chapter 9

Once Steve and I were allowed to see Jeff, the doctor told us we should still talk to him. "There's a good chance he can hear you but won't be able to respond. It's important, however, that he can at least sense you're with him."

Both of us started talking to him, trying to be positive. "You're gonna be fine, Buddy. The doctors are taking good care of you, and we're here," I said.

I found Mom in the hallway. Reality started to sink in, and I began shaking uncontrollably. "He's going to die. Jeff's dying! What are we going to do? He's going to die. My baby is dying. What possibly is there left? There's nothing left. He's dying."

My mother grabbed me. "Sue! You've got to get a hold of yourself! Jeff needs you to be okay." By this point, she was dragging me down the hall, speaking sternly, almost to the point of yelling at me. "You've got to pray. You've got to pray and give this to the Lord. He's the only one who can help Jeff. You have to give yourself over to God. You need to be strong and hold on. Cling to Him. We're going into the chapel now, and you are going to pray!"

"I don't know how. I don't know how to pray. I can't." I was falling apart, barely able to stand. She guided me into a pew and made me kneel down. "Then I'll pray with you. I'll pray out loud; you just follow or say what you want, and I'll sit here. I'll kneel with you."

The room was quiet and dark, although a few candles flickered. We were the only people there, which was probably a good thing. I was in dire straits, falling to pieces.

"Help. Help me. My Jeffy is dying. My baby's dying. Help him live. I'm going crazy. Help me. Dear Lord, help me!" Over and over, I repeated these words. Mom and I knelt there for quite a while, and the longer we stayed, the more I became capable of getting a few more words out. A little less shaking. A little less fragile.

I'd been raised in the Presbyterian church where my parents had both been involved, giving me a knowledge of who God was. Then I became a teenager and would only attend sporadically. Eventually, attendance stopped altogether. I knew enough to realize I hadn't been "born again," and though I'd never taken that step, I did start thinking about it more as I got older.

Now, kneeling with Mom, she kept saying, "You've got to give your life over to the Lord; you've got to." She was one strong lady who knew the Bible and had a deep belief system. I'd watched her face tragedy head-on and knew that the reason she'd been able to survive and come out strong was because of her faith.

Taking a deep breath, I said a simple prayer. "Dear God in heaven, I give myself to you. Please come into my life." There were no burning bushes, no lightning or thunderbolts. But I was able to stand on my own two feet and walked by myself back to the intensive care unit with Mom next to me.

Chapter 10

I noticed Jeff lay still with no expression on his face. His eyes, though slightly open, weren't moving or showing any type of reaction. I longed to touch him, but all the wires and contraptions surrounding him made it difficult. Then I found that by reaching across a cord or two, my hand could make contact with part of his arm. So, I massaged that area of his body while talking to him softly.

He didn't react when pricked with a pin. Nothing they tried aroused him. But, still, I was determined to continue touching and talking to him. It took all my strength to stay present and not give in to the tears that wanted to fall or to stave off the dreadful thoughts trying to take over my mind. Before I knew it, my time in Jeff's room was over, and it would be Steve's turn.

"Sue," my husband said to me, "you're as stiff as a board. You look like you're going to break in half." He was right. That's exactly how I felt - like a broken glass about to shatter into small, tiny pieces.

Next to me, my mother said, "Deep breaths. Bad air out; good air in. Take a moment at a time; that's all you're capable of doing right now." She was the person Steve and I held onto the tightest. Her life had been full of loss and grief, including my father's death at the age of thirty-three and that of her twenty-two-year-old son a few years earlier when he died in a motorcycle accident. She knew firsthand how grief could get its grip on you. Yes, Mom was our rock. We leaned on her for strength, prayer, hope, and love.

I looked around the lobby. The entire family was there. I saw my sister and brother as well as all of my in-laws. Also, good friends had arrived to support us. So many people had taken time out of their busy lives to be here. Their outpouring of love was humbling.

That night I slept for the first time. When I awoke in the morning, I was calm and peaceful.

The deep, engulfing ache had disappeared, along with my trembling. Beyond understanding, I knew it had to be a gift from God reassuring me I wasn't alone.

Prayer became my constant companion. It was getting easier to express my deepest desires. I begged God to heal my boy, to take away any pain he was experiencing, and for my continued peace of mind during this hell we were living through. In other words, I was praying for miracles. If I wasn't with Jeff, I'd be in the chapel either with Mom or by myself. It's no exaggeration to say that every fifteen minutes, I'd be at the altar pouring out my heart to God.

We made a pact as a family. There would be no sadness when our turn came to be with Jeff. We wanted to be positive and loving, to talk only about things familiar to him. Steve had turned on the television in his room so that football could enter his subconscious. Still, no response.

My prayers grew more substantial, and I'd sit in the chapel, unaware of anything else going on around me. During this time, something inexplicable occurred. I'm not sure exactly how or why, but I saw three spirits in front of me. There were no facial characteristics or distinct features, just an outline of three robed beings. But in my heart, there was no question Jesus sat in the middle. Though unable to humanly understand this, there was no denying the presence of God.

I have no idea how long I sat there, but my entire body became warm. Jesus stood next to me, and I felt led to stand up with Him. We left the chapel together, went down the hall, and back to Jeff's room. I laid my hand on my son's leg next to Jesus's. An incomprehensible, perfect love filled me. Then, the vision disappeared. I returned to the waiting room, telling no one about what had just happened.

Soon after sitting down, we noticed the doctor go into Jeff's room. Before long, he came back to us. "You won't believe this. Jeff's moving! He seems to be coming out of the coma and has even responded to pinpricks."

We were all thrilled beyond words. The doctor explained we should pick up the pace of being with him and continue talking in his presence. I rubbed the little patch of Jeff's arm where I could touch his skin, telling him how much he was loved.

"Jeff. Jeff. Please talk to me. Open your eyes - come back to us. We're all waiting to see you." Steve and I talked about Christmas coming soon and that we couldn't wait to celebrate with him.

The family now had the freedom to come and go, and it filled each one of us with increasing hope.

Chapter 11

His ability to respond continued throughout that day. The next morning, standing alone with him, I noticed tears running down his cheeks. Strange. I ran to tell my family, but none of us could decide what it meant.

Within a few minutes, Jeff's features changed for the worse. His face started drooping, and there were no more tears. Deep within, I knew my son had just said goodbye. But accepting it was another matter.

The next time the doctor examined him, he told us Jeff had fallen back into a deep coma.

Steve took my arm, guiding me into the hallway. "You have to be prepared that Jeff's not going to make it and be willing to let go, Sue. He's going to die."

Screaming at my husband, I pounded on his chest, over and over again. "How dare you? If you can't believe - if you're unable to hope with me and have faith - stay away from me. I don't need your negative feelings." I ran from him, into the chapel, and started yelling at God.

"How dare you give me hope and then yank it away from me? I was sure you'd healed him. What are you doing? I don't understand!"

I continued ranting for a few minutes until my mom came and got me. She said the doctors had inserted a catheter into Jeff's heart to control the heartbeat as well as a tube to drain the fluid from his lungs. It was at that moment I could see my boy's face had changed radically. There was no denying he couldn't hear me.

"Please, dear Lord Jesus, don't let him be afraid. Please don't let him feel the fear or anger I have or know that grief has its hold on me. I beg You to just be with him." I knelt at Jeff's bed, sobbing, my hands covering my face.

"Sue, go take a break," one of the nurses gently said. I knew that's what I should do, but no break could make all this go away, which is what I needed. Still, I stepped out of the room for a few moments taking deep breaths to calm myself. Turning around, I stopped in my tracks. The nurses were changing Jeff's bandages. His bare head was exposed, displaying the incision that went from ear-to-ear. I gasped, feeling heat flash across my face.

Another scan had to be done, which showed there was no brain activity at all. The doctor talked to us, explaining what that meant, and I knew we had to make a difficult decision.

Steve and I went to the cafeteria to be alone and talk about the one thing we didn't want to discuss. Should we tell the doctor to take Jeff off life support? We didn't want him to be in pain any longer, but the thought of him no longer being with us caused pure anguish. We talked for a few minutes and then decided that if the next brain scan showed nothing, we'd have our answer.

Chapter 12

The following day was the sixth day of Jeff being in a coma. We knew in our hearts as we approached his bed that even though the machines were keeping him alive, he'd already left us. As soon as the doctor rolled Jeff into imaging, we made our way to the little room off the ICU to wait for the results.

I had closed my eyes to say a prayer, and when I opened them, Dr. Haravey stood in front of us. Leaning closely in towards Steve and me, he softly stated, "The scan was black - Nothing was there. I'm so, so sorry. No parent should ever have to face the kind of pain both of you are going through." There were tears in the doctor's eyes as he continued, "Clinically, Jeff is dead. I have to ask what you want to do. Does he continue on life support, or do we disconnect the machines that are keeping him alive?"

The roaring in my head made it impossible to understand the doctor's words, but instinctively, I knew there was a choice to be made. I looked at Steve when he grabbed my leg. "Sue, what are we going to do?" I patted his hand, trying to be of some comfort.

It took me a moment to speak. "You know, doctor, I could ask a million questions."

He nodded.

"But I won't." With my head hanging, I said, "Take him off life support."

"Jeff's gone." Dr. Haravey spoke quietly. It was just after 3:00 p.m., December 6, 1977.

The three of us were silent; the feeling of defeat palpable. Eventually, Steve asked, "can we see him?"

We were hand-in-hand while telling our boy goodbye. The walls seemed to be closing in on me, and I turned around and rushed out of the room.

Dear Danny

I started wailing, and Steve grabbed hold of me. We stood embracing until my dear husband picked me up in his arms and carried me to the car. I simply couldn't put one foot in front of the other. Still, even with all the turmoil, I could feel Jeff's spirit around me.

Chapter 13

Once home, I went straight upstairs to Jeff's room and fell onto his bed, clutching the soft quilt he slept with every night. I buried my face in it and shook uncontrollably with deep, guttural sobs. Sheer torment flooded every fiber of my being. I had an awareness that Steve and Mom took turns sitting with me as long as they could bear my raw emotions.

I cried and cried and cried and cried until exhaustion took over, and I eventually fell asleep.

Once I opened my eyes, I could tell the sun had gone down. I noticed the bedroom door was open enough for me to see the light shine through. Mom stood outside the door, and I mumbled for her to come in. She sat down next to me, gently rubbing my back.

"Oh, sweetheart, I'm so, so sorry. There's nothing else in this world that hurts more than losing a child. If only I could take your pain away." A few minutes passed before she said, "You've been in here for quite a few hours. Do you think you're up to coming downstairs and getting a bite to eat?"

I sighed deeply. "I don't know, Mom. I'm not sure if I can even stand up."

"Let's give it a try. You can lean on me; we'll walk slowly."

My eyes had a difficult time adjusting to the bright light. Mom held onto me, and we took the stairs one step at a time. When we reached the bottom, my gaze swept the room. Touched by seeing so many family members, I fought the tears and sat down next to Steve. He pulled me close, and I grasped his hand.

"Sue, we have sandwiches that your sister brought," my mom called out from the kitchen. "They're also chips and salsa, soft drinks, and the coffee's ready. What do you think?"

"Coffee would be nice, and could you put sugar and milk in it?"

"No problem. Hey, how about an apple? I'll slice it if you like."

Nodding my head, Steve answered for me. "Yeah, that'd be great."

The phone rang, and Dad picked up the receiver. It was Dr. Haravey. "Just checking on everyone. How's Sue doing?" he asked.

"She cried herself to sleep shortly after we got home and just now got up. She's sitting with all of us trying to eat a little something."

"Do you have some kind of a sleeping aid? She's going to need it."

Dad told him he'd take a look but was sure he could find something in the medicine cabinet. Whatever it was he found helped me make it through the night without waking up.

The next day, others handled the funeral arrangements. I could barely move from one room to the next, let alone set foot outside. Later that day, Steve and I sat together, deciding what to put on Jeff's headstone. We chose a bright little star for the top and an image of a football on the bottom. His name and the dates of his birth and death were in the middle. Trees surrounded a beautiful plot, so we decided on it for our son's final resting place. Because it was in a new children's area, there were even little bunnies hopping around.

I can't tell you much about the next few days, except that his funeral took place on December 10th, in a lovely glass chapel. One of the songs I chose was, "You Light Up My Life." I began shaking and crying when I heard the lyrics, but Steve's dad started trying to catch my attention.

"Sue, turn around. You need to look out the window. The sunlight just came out from behind the clouds." It had been raining all day up until that moment. He went on, "Look at the stained glass windows. It looks like one large sunray beaming down onto Jeff." Amazed at the sight, a moment's peace encompassed me. There was no doubt that my boy was in heaven, surrounded by love.

Chapter 14

Steve returned to work about a week after the funeral. My boss approved of me taking the next month off, for which I was grateful since there was no possible way I could concentrate on anything, let alone my job.

I didn't want to get out of bed or get dressed. Even more problematic was eating, but I realized I had to try. If I gave up on life, my family would suffer even more than they were already. Turning to my one source of peace, I prayed continuously. Jesus lifted me daily, even hourly, and I knew He'd never leave my side.

It soon became necessary to interact with other people, which brought on a new level of stress. It seemed everyone was clueless as to my feelings or how to react to me. My friends shied away most of the time. If only

I could climb into a hole and never have to talk to anyone again, I'd be happy. How was it possible for the sun to rise and set every day? My world had been torn to shreds, and yet, the lives of other people went on as usual. It boggled my mind.

Time went by slowly. The house felt empty without Jeff, and the silence was deafening. In a sense, this helped in my process of preparing to return to work. Perhaps being around co-workers would help take the edge off some of my loneliness.

Since I wasn't sure what to expect that first day back, it helped when my office manager called me at home a few days before my scheduled return.

"Sue," she said, "I know that it's going to be difficult, but don't forget everybody here cares about you. If you find yourself needing anything at all, please don't hesitate to let someone know. What are your thoughts about working half-days for the first couple of weeks? Maybe kind of easing into it would help."

"That would be nice."

"Some of us were wondering if you'd like to go to lunch the day before starting back."

"Umm, I'm not sure if I want to do that. I'm afraid it would feel like being put in the spotlight, and that would make me uncomfortable," I answered slowly.

"We'll let the idea go for now, but if you change your mind, give me a call."

Kathy was a kind person, and I knew she wanted to make it as easy for me as possible. I recalled when my brother died, and I was trying to get back to a routine. People I worked with kept their distance and were uncomfortable around me. While I wasn't happy with that reaction, I was also aware that I didn't want everyone falling all over me, either. I mentioned this to Kathy.

"Well, let me tell you that several of your co-workers have asked me how they should approach you. I told them that I thought they should acknowledge you and welcome you back but not go overboard. Is there anything else you think should or shouldn't be done?"

"No, it's great advice. Thanks for that."

I felt uneasy walking into work that first day but appreciated the love and respect given me.

There were days when I cried all the way to work and back home again, but I tried not to bring my emotions with me. Steve was in his own pain, so I made an effort to at least take care of those things that had to be done, like making dinner and doing laundry. We stopped sitting at the dining table and began eating on TV trays in front of the television. Anything to change our routine and not have to face the fact there were only two place settings where there should have been three.

Every little thing was different. When I washed clothes, I no longer needed to use a stain remover because there were no dirty shirts or pants of Jeff's that needed washing. Going to the market brought with it loneliness that felt tangible. And when walking through the cereal aisle, no little boy was bugging me to buy Frosted Flakes or Sugar Pops. I missed not having Jeff there to beg for more cookies or other treats he loved, even though I'd complained to Steve about it in the past.

Chapter 15

About a year passed when my little brother, Billy, mentioned that he missed me. We were walking together in a park close to home.

"But, Billy, I haven't gone anywhere. I'm right here."

"You're here physically maybe, but not in any other way. I miss my sister who used to laugh and enjoy life. The sister who liked to have fun and didn't seem to have a care in the world. The one person in my life I've always been able to talk to about anything."

On the surface, I knew I wasn't the only one who missed Jeff but believed the pain others felt didn't come close to mine. My brother's words stunned me. Had I built a wall separating me from all the people in my life who were only trying to help? Was my family hurting because of my inability to think about them and their feelings?

Yes, that's exactly what I've done — pushed everyone away.

"Billy, please forgive me. My thoughts have only been about myself, and I don't want to be like that. I completely ignored the fact that you and Jeff had a close relationship. You must miss him like crazy." Even with six years between them, they were like best friends. Rarely did you see one without the other.

"I promise never to do that again. If we go through more hard times, we'll be in it together." I pulled him into a bear hug and held him close. As brother and sister, we sat down on a bench, and he began pouring his heart out to me.

Afterward, I began thinking about all the people in my life. *Wow, they not only lost Jeff, but me, too.* Including my parents and other siblings, the good friends I'd pushed away when all they wanted to do was reach out to me. *And Steve. Had I done the same thing to him?*

Steve confessed that he, too, missed me, that I no longer acted like the girl he'd married. "When was the last time you touched me lovingly? I've held it in because I didn't want you to hurt more than you already do, but it's gotten old."

Through God's grace and help, I began working on the relationship with him and other people in my life. Slowly but surely, my old self broke through, and joy is no longer a stranger to me. There's a long road ahead, but instead of dreading it, I'm starting to look forward to the future. After all, I've lived through the heartwrenching pain of losing a child. What could stop me now?

PART II
THE REST OF THE STORY

Chapter 16

I'll never forget the day in December 1977 when Steve called.

"Shari. Something horrible happened." He went on to tell me about Jeff's accident, which occurred when one of his friends impishly pushed a skateboard in front of him and his fast-approaching bike.

"His intent wasn't malicious; just a kid being a kid. But Jeff flew over the handlebars, landing on his head," Steve replied to my question of what happened.

"Oh, my Lord! Is he okay?"

A moment passed before Steve could choke out the words, "He died, Shari. He died."

"No, Steve, no. It can't be. Not Jeff." I was wiping away the tears as quickly as they ran down my cheeks. "Oh, my gosh. Is Sue okay?"

Did I really say that? What was I thinking? Of course, she wasn't okay.

"No, she's not. She cries constantly and can barely get out of bed. It's so hard on both of us, Shari. I don't know what to do." Then there was silence, both of us wordlessly mourning the loss of an extraordinary little boy.

"I - we - wanted you to know his funeral will be on December 10th. Don't worry if you can't make it."

"Of course, I'll be there. But is there anything at all I can do for you guys before that? Anything?"

Steve answered, "Not that I can think of. We have relatives who are helping out a lot, and everything is taken care of, at least as of right now." After he and I talked for a few more minutes, I hung up the phone, frozen in place. I felt like a truck had hit me.

Chapter 17

Memories of Sue and our friendship flooded my mind. *Had it only been four years since we first met? It seemed so much longer than that.*

I remember that September day in 1973 when I got off the elevator on the 4th floor where my new job awaited me. Anxious, I took a deep breath, willing myself to calm down. Two weeks before that, I'd left a large, impersonal insurance company for more money and better opportunities at a smaller workplace. I hoped people here would be friendlier.

My new department manager welcomed me, and after a few minutes of small talk, he took me to Sue's desk and introduced us. He explained she would be taking me around to meet my new co-workers and help me become familiar with the company's layout.

I could sense a warmth about Sue and I felt at ease right away.

"I'm so glad to meet you, Shari. I think you'll like it here - I know I do. The people are friendly, and I get the feeling you're gonna fit right in."

It turned out she was right, and my initial thought that we might become friends was also true. Although our desks were on opposite ends of the office, our paths crossed often, and rarely did we miss having lunch together.

Our friendship stretched beyond the office when we started to spend time together on weekends. We introduced our husbands, and soon we all became close. Sue had a little four-year-old boy who I fell in love with the first time I met him. Jeff was cute, funny, and mature beyond his years. Mother and son adored each other, and it was a joy being in their company.

I became a mother in 1976; I only hoped my baby would turn out to be a great kid, like Jeff. Sue and I went shopping towards the end of my pregnancy.

There were multiple necessities for babies that she pointed out, most foreign to me. She and I had such fun that day in the mall, going from store-to-store all the while laughing until our sides ached. By the end of the day, I was exhausted, but it had been more than worth it.

I had a boy, Josh, and couldn't have been happier in my new role. It was mainly through Sue's help that I learned about being a mom and I loved staying at home with my baby.

On a summer day in 1977, Sue called to tell me her regular babysitter was going on vacation and wondered if I'd be able to watch Jeff for a couple of weeks. I jumped at the chance.

"Shari, you remember my niece, Misty, right? She's just a month older than Josh. She loves it whenever Jeff is around. Her little face lights up when he enters the room, and she can't take her eyes off of him. I bet Josh will have the same reaction."

Jeff loved books and enjoyed reading to my baby, who was captivated by his new eight-year-old friend. We enjoyed the walks we took together in my neighborhood and were entertained by birds chirping from the tall shade trees that surrounded the area. Jeff would push the stroller with me next to him, and we'd talk and talk.

His questions were never-ending. "Is the moon made out of cheese, and is there a man in it?" Before taking a breath, he'd thought of something else to ask, like, "Do you know why cows and sheep sleep standing up? Wow, Shari, look at all those ants crossing the sidewalk. They must like their leader, 'cause they're all following him." On and on he went, putting a smile on my face. After the walk, it would be time for Josh's nap and for Jeff to lay on my bed and read, which inevitably brought more questions.

It was difficult saying goodbye once Sue's babysitter returned, but I knew there'd be more good times down the road for us to spend together.

The next four months flew by, and then I received the heartwrenching phone call from Steve.

Stunned, I couldn't believe I'd never see Jeff again.

Chapter 18

Three years passed. Sue and I had occasional telephone conversations and saw each other sporadically. But life has a habit of getting in the way, and before you know it, things have changed, making it challenging to keep up with old friends.

In the spring of 1980, I found myself in need of a full-time job. The first person I thought to call was Sue. After we exchanged pleasantries, I explained why I'd called.

"Do you happen to know of any openings there might be at your firm?"

"Maybe. I think there's an entry-level position for a secretary they want to fill. Have you ever worked in the legal field?"

I hadn't but was willing to learn. Sue said she'd talk to the office manager and get back to me. Her boss called me that afternoon and set up an interview. One week later, I started my new job. The frosting on the cake was that Sue and I worked together again.

Her personality had changed after losing Jeff, but she was still able to put a smile on her face. I couldn't help but admire her. One day she told me she was afraid I was putting her on a pedestal. I had to agree with her and told her so.

Quiet for a moment, she asked, "Why would you do that?"

"Sue, you've been through the worst of the worst. I realize the first couple of years after Jeff died were dreadful for you, but you survived. I look up to you more than anyone else I know and want to emulate you."

"Oh, please don't do that. It's still difficult for me to get out of bed every day, and you can find me crying in the bathroom here at work too many times to count. I simply take a deep breath and put one foot in front of the other," she explained.

"Which is what I'm talking about. I guess the saying 'what doesn't kill you makes you stronger' fits you like a T."

"The problem with being put on a pedestal is, if you fall, it's a long way down."

Sadly, her words would prove to be prophetic.

Chapter 19

For quite a few months, I'd been tossing the idea around in my head to write Jeff's story. I believed it had a message that many people could relate to, plus I wanted to do something to honor my dear friend and her son. When I approached Sue with the idea, her reaction was positive. We talked for a while about it, and she answered many of the questions I had. We decided I'd write a few pages for her to read to help make up her mind whether this was something she wanted done.

It only took me a few days to get something down on paper, and when I gave it to her, tears welled up in her eyes. "Thanks for doing this, Shari. It means a lot to me that you would want to remember my boy like this."

Her reaction touched my heart, and I couldn't wait for her to read it.

We sat down to eat lunch together a few days later. Sue told me she needed to talk about the story. "I love what you've done so far, and I've made notes about several things," she said, handing it back to me. "But the more I think about it, the more I believe this is something I myself, should write. What are your thoughts?"

Though surprised by what she told me, I couldn't help but agree. After all, it *was* her story, even though I did feel a bit disappointed that I wouldn't be the person to tell it. Then I noticed the look on her face. Her relief that she hadn't hurt my feelings was apparent.

"Will you let me read it when you've finished?"

"I wouldn't have it any other way," she said.

Probably six months later, she gave me her draft. It became clear that getting her thoughts and feelings down on paper had been cathartic for her. Going through the exercise of writing about the tragedy proved helpful in Sue's healing process. She seemed to walk a little taller and exuded more confidence than I'd noticed in a long time.

Nothing more was ever mentioned about what she wrote by either of us again. Seemingly, Sue had attained her purpose of writing the story, and we didn't need to discuss it any further. It wouldn't come to mind until many years later when I discovered my copy of her manuscript.

Chapter 20

Sue's niece, Misty, was born in March 1976, our country's bicentennial. Because Josh arrived just a month later, Sue and I went a little crazy buying red, white and blue outfits. Whether or not we were celebrating our country's 200th birthday, we'd been given an excuse to shop.

Misty's mother was only 20 years old when she was born. Even though not prepared for motherhood, she tried. But when Misty was diagnosed with lupus, a possibly fatal disease, it was more than she could handle.

Sue's mom and dad became their granddaughter's caregivers. However, they weren't as young as they used to be, which concerned Sue. She approached her mother with the prospect of changing things around.

"Mom, I think what you're doing is incredible, but I've watched and can see that it's not easy for you to take care of a six-year-old. I know from experience how rough it can be. Steve and I have talked it over, and we want Misty to live with us."

"Absolutely not! It hasn't been that long since Jeffy died, and now we've been told that Misty may not live long. What would that do to you?"

"I won't lie; it'd be hard, but the circumstances are different from Jeff's. A good part of my grief over losing him stemmed from the shock of it all. Steve and I enjoyed being parents and would love to be her guardians," said Sue.

"I know Misty spends a lot of time at your house, but having her on a full-time basis is much different."

"Be honest with me, Mom. Haven't you noticed you're moving around a lot slower than you used to? It hurts to see you have such difficulty trying to keep up with an active little girl every day. And Dad's having the same issues. Please consider our offer."

Shaking her head, Audrey walked away, leaving Sue standing alone.

It didn't take her mom long to relent, knowing her daughter was right. What helped her decide was her husband's noticeable decline in health. "All right, Sue, you win. But I'm not at all happy about it."

"Thank you! Thank you so much. We're the right age to be raising a child, and Steve and I both want to do it. As far as the lupus is concerned, you and I both know doctors have been wrong before."

Chapter 21

Sue was right. Having Misty in their lives turned out to be the right decision for everyone. Miraculously, the lupus disappeared. Whether it was because of the many prayers offered on Misty's behalf - as believed by many, including Sue - the doctors had no medical explanation of why it was gone.

Unfortunately, Sue and Steve's marriage didn't fare as well. They were able to make a go of it for the first few years after Jeff's death, but when Steve started spending most of his time away from home, Sue's loneliness and depression was all-consuming. Communication between the two of them became non-existent, and eventually, they divorced.

Though unable to adopt Misty legally because of finances, Sue considered her a daughter. Now it was more important than ever that the two of them stay together.

Time went by, and Sue ran into an old flame from her high school years. Larry was from the same neighborhood that Sue had grown up in (and where her parents still lived), so it wasn't a surprise when their paths crossed. He'd been her first love, and Sue had never completely gotten over him. They talked on the phone for hours on end, and as the sparks flew, the couple's relationship was renewed. But there was something Sue had kept from Larry since high school.

Jeff was his son.

When finding out at sixteen that she was pregnant, her decision to tell no one who the father was seemed appropriate. At that time, Larry was a senior and had accepted a scholarship to play college golf. In no time at all, he'd be leaving. Sue remembered their conversation from that day

"It's unbelievable. Who'd have ever thought this would happen? Think about it. Me, in college, getting to do what I love best! My parents couldn't be happier." Larry was as excited as a little kid.

"I'm happy for you, but we'd be living in different states. I love you and can't stand the idea of us being so far apart from each other," Sue said.

"But you have to think about what it could mean for us. I might become a professional golfer. Wouldn't that be great?"

Chapter 22

Sue had to agree. But now this. A baby. No way could she be responsible for shattering Larry's dreams.

So, I just won't tell him. It'll be easy to convince James that the baby is his since we just broke up from our short summer romance. And I'll also tell him I don't want anything from him; that he should go and live his life. Yeah, that'll work. The important thing is that Larry never finds out.

Little did Sue know that her mother would insist on her marrying James after she refused to have an abortion. Audrey believed no man would ever accept someone else's baby and was adamant in her stance. Being so young, Sue didn't have a choice in the matter. That short-lived union - in every sense a sham - ended in divorce within months.

Now, while she and Larry walked down the street hand-in-hand, Sue stopped and took a deep breath. "Can we go back to my house? I have something important we need to talk about."

Larry answered, "I think I know what it is - -"

Interrupting him, Sue said, "You couldn't possibly - -"

Now it was his turn to break in. "Jeff was my son, wasn't he?"

She stared at him. "How - how did you know?"

"I think I've always known but wouldn't admit it. I did hear from friends that you'd had a baby. When I did the math, I had an inkling he might be mine. But I figured things were fine the way they were. I went on with my life and got married after the golf thing fell through. I figured if you wanted to tell me, you would. And, besides, what if it turned out I was wrong? You had your own life, and I wasn't a part of it."

"How long did your marriage last? I know you have a couple of kids."

"Long enough for us to have the two girls. We both had some issues that wouldn't go away, and before too many years went by, we split up."

"Did you know I got married to another guy before Steve and I met? He turned out to be a real loser and treated Jeff badly, so it didn't last long."

Larry nodded and told her he'd found out about it from a friend. They talked into the night.

In 1984 the couple got married in Larry's backyard. I went to their wedding and couldn't help but shed a few tears, especially when his two daughters and Misty sang a beautiful love song together, dedicating it to the happy couple. Oh, and by the way, Sue and Larry adopted Misty in 1988.

Chapter 23

Life had its ups and downs for this blended family. Whenever two households are combined, it can be difficult at best. Theirs was no exception, especially with three teenage girls now living under one roof. Larry's daughters had a difficult time not resenting Sue, while she, on the other hand, wanted to mother them. But they already had a mom. There were a lot of slammed doors and hurt feelings between the three of them.

The biggest problem in recent years was Sue's erratic highs and lows, a continuing depression, together with ongoing anger. It felt like a stormcloud hung over them all. Counseling didn't work, and finally, after more than ten years of walking on eggshells, the family imploded. Sue and Misty left the family in 1994.

Post Traumatic Stress Disorder (PTSD) wasn't recognized in those days, but there's no denying that Sue displayed all the signs. Losing Jeff had taken its toll on her. Add to that the divorces, and it's no surprise she had mental issues. Perhaps if she had been willing to seek counseling, things might have been different. But whenever confronted, Sue insisted nothing was wrong with her.

Sue's DNA gave her a proclivity towards emotional problems. Her mother and grandmother had lived complex lives, and they both longed for love. Audrey's first husband (Sue's father) had his problems, but there was no question about how much he loved his family. At thirty-three, he died, having been diagnosed with scleroderma (a group of rare, untreatable diseases that affect people between thirty and fifty).

Knowing he wouldn't live a long life, he wanted to ensure his wife and three children would be cared for. He paid off the car and house, leaving the family debt-free. But in her grief and loneliness, Audrey married shortly after her husband's death, which turned out to be a mistake. Being an abuser, Sue's stepfather made life miserable for everyone around him, and the marriage ended in divorce.

Then, Frank came along, and, although not perfect, Audrey now had a decent marriage. He loved the kids as his own, and Sue considered him to be her father.

All this to say, my friend leaned naturally towards emotional problems, including denial and control.

Chapter 24

In January 1995, Misty and Sue packed their bags and moved to Hawaii. Since Misty's birth father was Hawaiian, it wasn't a surprise to anyone. It's where Misty's roots lay, and Sue was more than happy to leave California.

They established a life in Kauai with Sue finding work at a restaurant and Misty going to college. Their lives were stress-free, and they enjoyed their well-earned happiness. Within the first year of living in Hawaii, Misty met the man who would become her husband. Both enjoyed basketball, and it was on a public court that the two of them discovered each other. Neither of them had been looking for that special person, but that's precisely what happened.

Now that Misty was in a serious relationship, Sue decided she wanted the same.

She and her boyfriend, Brian, had been dating only a few months, and Misty thought the couple shouldn't rush into things.

"Sue, you've only been together four months. Four short months," Misty said. "That isn't enough time to really know someone. At the very least, you could live together for a year or so and then see how you feel."

"Live together? There's no way I'd do that. It's against my morals. And what do you think my mother would say?" Sue wouldn't listen to reason, so there were two weddings in February 1997.

Sue became pregnant with Danny right away. She and Brian were thrilled even though she was now in her forties, and their relationship was rocky.

"I'm going to be a mom again!" Tears welled up in her eyes as she told Brian the good news. "I can't believe it. It's such a miracle!"

"And I'm going to be a dad. My first kid. Do you think it'll be a boy?"

The only thing on Sue's mind was that she'd have another child to love. Girl or boy? It didn't matter to her.

The lack of jobs in Hawaii for both Brian and Misty's husband, Keoni, led the two couples back to California, where Danny was born on April 1, 1998. Sue doted on her son, never letting him out of her sight. Danny was a happy baby, always laughing as Sue plied him with hugs and kisses. Now, she was confident her life had turned around, and all would be well.

Chapter 25

Life in California seemed to be going well. Sue and Brian worked on their marriage and were hopeful they'd grow old together. Money was still tight, but the family of three found ways to have fun.

Sue was running errands one afternoon when she received a phone call from a friend of Brian's.

"Hey, Randy. How's it going? You and Brian having a good day?"

The two friends hadn't seen each other in a while, so they'd planned a day together just hanging out.

Randy sounded out of breath.

"What's going on? Did something happen?" Sue asked him.

"Brian collapsed while we were playing pool here at my house. He didn't respond to me when I tried talking to him, so I called the paramedics. They're rushing him to the hospital right now. I have no clue what's going on. I'm so sorry, Sue."

"Which hospital?" she shouted into her phone.

Randy told her, and she rushed to her husband's side.

They called it the widowmaker.

"But he's only forty-years-old! That's way too young to have a heart attack and die," screamed Sue at the doctors standing in front of her. "What am I going to do?" Distraught, she collapsed into a chair.

Danny was eighteen-months-old and now fatherless. He also lost his mother that day - if not physically, certainly emotionally. Sue immediately went into survival mode. Misty told friends that she acted like a robot. Her movements were automatic, without feeling. She pushed away anyone who tried to comfort her. When Misty attempted to help out with Danny, Sue wouldn't let her, saying that as his mother, only she could care for him. No one else. But the truth of it was, she could barely function, even when it came to her son.

"Sue, you have to get help," Misty told her time and again. "You're living through unimaginable agony. No one could stay sane after all you've been through."

"No. I'm fine. I'm taking care of my baby, and that's all I need to do."

"I wouldn't call it 'taking care of your baby,' Sue. You ignore him, and when you do hold him, it's hardly for more than a couple of minutes."

"I'm doing the best I can. Leave me alone."

Although Sue and Brian had bought a house shortly after moving to California, she spent all her time at Misty and Keoni's since her husband's death. Misty's hands were already full taking care of her young daughters while her husband worked long hours, yet she couldn't refuse Sue with her many needs.

Sue moved around a lot over the next few years but always seemed to wind up on Misty's doorstep. When Danny was old enough to go to kindergarten, Misty made sure he would be going to the same school as her daughters. Sue didn't have a problem with this, but by the following year, she refused for him to leave her side. All too often, the two women would end up in screaming matches.

"No, he isn't going," yelled Sue.

"What do you mean, he's not going? Of course, Danny's going to school. For one thing, it's the law. Aside from that, don't you want him to learn and grow up to be a normal kid?"

"I can teach him all that he needs to know. He's my son, and you don't have anything to say about it."

"When the two of you are living here with us, I do have something to say about it!" Frustrated, Misty threw down the kitchen towel she was holding and stormed off into the living room.

"Fine. Go ahead and enroll him. But don't expect me to get him there."

Chapter 26

April was quickly approaching, and Danny would be six-years-old. "Let's throw him a birthday party," Sue excitedly said to Misty. "I remember that when Jeff was eight, Steve and I threw him a party, and it was the best day ever!"

Although Sue wouldn't see a doctor, she exhibited all the signs of being bipolar. One day she was depressed and wouldn't speak to anyone, including Danny, and the next - well, she wanted to have a party.

Misty talked to Keoni about it. "What do you think? Should we plan something? Lord only knows what kind of mood she'll be in that day."

"We need to think of Danny and how much it would mean to him. Even if Sue refuses to be involved that day, you and I can pull it off. I say we invite the neighborhood kids and his classmates for a party in our backyard," said Keoni.

Misty agreed. It would be wonderful to watch Danny have fun with his friends. The weather on the morning of April 1, 2004, turned out to be lovely. Blowing up balloons and hanging streamers, Misty and Keoni were hard at work when Sue stepped outside.

"What are you doing?" she yelled to the couple.

"Getting ready for Danny's birthday party. Remember, it's this afternoon," Misty answered.

"Oh. Yeah. Well, I forgot, and besides, I don't feel so good. I'm going back to bed."

"No surprise there," Misty mumbled to her husband. He nodded in agreement as he continued blowing up balloons.

The party was a hit, and Danny had a great time. He was so busy enjoying himself that he hadn't been aware of his mom's absence. But everyone else was. A few of Sue's friends had asked Misty about her, who explained Sue was sick in bed. More than one of them tried to talk to her, but she wouldn't let anyone in her room.

After the party was over, Misty went to check on her. She noticed Sue's swollen face; clearly, she was in quite a bit of pain.

"What's going on, Sue?

Although it was difficult for her to talk, she pointed to her face and groaned, "My mouth hurts."

"Let me take you to the doctor."

"No. No way," refused Sue. "Be better in the morning. Go 'way."

Knowing there was no use arguing, Misty closed the door behind her and went to help Danny get ready for bed.

Later, Misty would recall a significant change in Sue that day. She became even more noncommunicative and belligerent than she had been in recent years.

"You know," Misty commented to Keoni one day, "I think on top of having a badly infected tooth, she might have also had a stroke of some kind."

"We'll never know, will we, since she refuses to talk to anyone about it or go see a doctor." Keoni had had enough. But he knew how important Sue was to Misty, so he said nothing else.

Chapter 27

Over the next few years, Sue and Danny moved from place to place, including motels, friends' or relatives' homes, and occasionally lived on the streets. Then the day came when the two of them wound up on Misty's doorstep unannounced once again.

"I don't know what else to do," Misty cried to Keoni. "There's an innocent minor involved here, and he doesn't deserve this."

"I know, and I agree, but enough is enough. The woman needs help."

Misty once again contacted the authorities reporting that Sue was neglecting Danny. Still, any time the police arrived to question her, Sue was able to pull off the appearance of being a normal, loving mom. She knew what they wanted to hear and said all the right things, avoiding any trouble. This scenario repeated itself time and again, and all the while, Danny suffered most.

While at Misty's, Sue's daily routine became one of sitting on a folding chair in the backyard and chain smoking for hours on end. Lost in her thoughts, she never spoke to anyone. So, when Misty woke up one morning and realized Sue had left with Danny, she was both relieved and worried.

Misty learned through the grapevine that Sue had taken Danny to the streets with her. It was a miserable existence, wandering from place to place. Money from Brian's social security benefits was electronically deposited into a bank account that Sue had kept open, which helped keep them fed.

When Danny was about sixteen, he called his aunt, begging to be able to come live with Misty and her family again. "I'm so sick of being homeless. I just can't do it anymore." Hearing the desperation in his voice broke her heart.

"Yes, Danny, you can come, but not your mother. Because she refuses to get help, she's no longer welcome here. My kids have been affected by her and her actions far too long. I'm not going to put up with it anymore. Plus, I'm confused because I know she receives money once a month, at least enough to rent a room. Why are you still living on the streets?"

"It makes no sense. I'm on her case all the time about it, but she seems to enjoy being homeless. Every time I threaten to leave, she tells me she'll kill herself if I go. But I don't want to continue living this way."

"She's manipulating you. Please, please, Danny, it's got to come from you. Call the police and turn her in," sighed Misty said.

For a moment, Danny was silent. Then, he whispered, "I can't do that to her. She's still my mom."

Misty told Keoni what was going on, and they jumped in their car. They found him on a street corner alone, his mother nowhere in sight. As soon as he opened the door and got in, there was a collective sigh of relief. Danny was going home.

Chapter 28

Danny was a welcome addition to their family. Without the drama Sue inherently brought with her, they could settle down to a routine. But Misty had difficulty relaxing, fearful that Sue might alert the police about her missing son during one of her lucid moments.

Misty carefully planned any routes they took outside the house to avoid Sue's known hangouts. Though she never questioned the decision to bring Danny back home, she knew Sue was well aware they didn't have legal guardianship, and it wouldn't take much for the police to become involved.

"I feel like I need to be able to see around corners or something," Misty mentioned to her husband. "My fear is we'll run into Sue, and she'll either grab him or demand to have him back."

"Well, that's a realistic concern, Misty," said Keoni. "But we can't live our lives being afraid of what could happen. Be careful, yes, but you've got to let it go. It's gonna drive you crazy."

Her wariness continued for about a year before she could let her guard down. Thankfully, there was no interference. Misty still held Sue lovingly in her heart, always prayerful that someday she would come to her right mind.

Four years went by without any contact from Sue. Occasionally, Misty would hear from a friend who had run into her and reported that she lived on the streets by herself. The conversations they had were nonsensical, and she never asked for help. Sue's life had spun completely out of control.

Chapter 29

Because there was no communication between them, Misty was unsure of where Sue might be any given day. She didn't dwell on it but couldn't help but wonder about Sue's safety and welfare. The fact of the matter was, though, that Sue did what she wanted to do, and there was no changing that fact.

In February 2019, Misty received a call from Larry, Sue's ex-husband. Right before that, there had been texts from her stepsisters to call their father. There was no doubt in Misty's mind that it had to be about Sue, and it wasn't going to be good.

"Misty, the San Juan Capistrano Police Department contacted me." He hesitated for a few moments. "I'm so sorry to have to tell you that Sue's body was discovered beind a local supermarket by a store employee."

It took her some time before she could speak. "Why do you think they notified you instead of me?"

"They told me they hadn't been able to reach you, and I guess they found a note or something in her belongings with my name and phone number."

Although not unexpected, it still astounded Misty that Sue's life was over. "If only she hadn't beern so darned stubborn," she said to Larry as they ended their conversation. "Maybe she could have lived a different life."

The coroner listed the cause of death to be emphysema.

No longer trapped by her demons, my dear friend is now at peace, fully encompassed by God's love.

Epilogue

Sue led a troublesome life. The unthinkable was thrown at her time and again, but in the end, she was her own worst enemy. Still, my life is richer having known her, and I consider it a blessing that our paths crossed so many years ago.

Misty and I met on numerous occasions for me to learn more about Sue's life. I'm grateful for her insight and willingness to share the good, the bad, and the ugly. Without her, Sue's story might never have been told.

When I asked Misty what she hoped would be accomplished by this book, she told me there were two things. First of all (and as mentioned in the Preface), her deepest wish is that you, Danny, could know more about your mom and understand the life she lived before you came along.

Secondly, Misty wants people to know she believes Sue might have sought help had she pressed her harder. "In hindsight, I wish I had gone to other family members and friends to band together and convince Sue to seek therapy. Mental illness is a real disease and affects millions of people. Yet, those who accept they have a problem can receive treatment. I hope that anyone who has a Sue in their life may be able to go that extra mile."

About the Author

Shari Riggs is the author of *Memories Matter*, a memoir of short stories about her life: from growing up in the 1960s in Southern California to adulthood and retirement. She lives in Orange County, California with her dog, Ella. Family is most important to Shari, including her six grandchildren of whom she couldn't be more proud.